## THE DREAM OF PEACE

The student was lost. He found himself angry on a regular basis. In general, people seemed to disappoint him, and life rarely seemed to turn out the way he expected it to turn out. One person in particular occupied a tremendous amount of space in his mind. This person hurt him a great deal, but anger covered his hurt (as it usually does for all of us). He was tired of being angry all the time, however, but he didn't know how to rid himself of it.

That evening, he asked for help. He shouted for it, actually. He let out his exhausting anger until he fell asleep. When he fell asleep, he dreamed.

And in the dream he met a wise man....

He said to the sage, "I'm tired of being a slave to anger. Help me to not be so angry anymore."

The wise man said:

"Anger is limbless and devoid of faculties: How then, do you allow it to reduce you to its slave?"

"I don't know," said the student, "I guess I never

thought of that." He hesitated, and then said, "People do stupid things that make me angry all the time, though."

The wise man smiled and replied, "People are supposed to treat us poorly from time to time. If people did not treat us poorly, then how could we learn patience?"

"I don't know," said the student, "I never thought of it in that way." He searched his mind for a moment and said, "But people criticize me for no reason at all. I've done nothing to them and I certainly don't ask for it!"

The guru replied, "You see people who criticize you as enemies, but criticism is a blessing because it helps us stay realistic about who we are."

"I guess it does," said the student, "I just get so angry at people who are ignorant!"

The wise man answered, "It's true that some people do mean things out of ignorance, but it is also true that others respond with anger. Who is to say who is faultless?"

"I hadn't considered that," replied the student, who then thought about the one person whose injustice has stuck with him the longest. He told the guru about the pain this person caused him, about the anger he had day and night about it. He told him how the pain and anger seemed to control his every thought now. "What do I do about that?" he asked.

The wise man took a long, deep breath. He smiled and seemed to fade away, but his voice was as clear as before: "Invite anger into your home if you will, but only as a guest. It cannot live in your home. Serve your guest the food you prepared before he arrived, and you will be in control of what you feed your guest. When you understand this much, you will find peace."

And he woke up. And so too, should we….

6

## VISION AND PATIENCE

Vision saw things that others didn't. When he was young, Vision's classmates would poke fun at his claiming to see things that were seemingly nonexistent. Regardless of what others said or did, however, Vision held to the things he saw.

Patience was friendly and generous. She was accepting, forgiving, and compassionate. No matter what others said or did, Patience exuded a kind and loving temperament.

When Vision met Patience he instantly knew the two of them would be together, but in his haste to fulfill what he saw, he made mistakes. Their relationship did not prosper immediately. Vision was brilliant but, as usual, he wanted things to happen quickly – and triumph over anything does not occur in that way.

Patience, on the other hand, was happily willing to watch their relationship and their love grow. Once Vision spent enough time with Patience, her steady ways, calmness, composure, and willingness to endure began to rub off on him. When it did, he saw her in a whole new way, and he began to put the right effort into their relationship. Their love, though not the mythical "love at first sight," has since become a kind of *ever-after* love in that it not only changed their own lives, but also the lives of countless others as well.

You see, legend has it that even to this day, the success of their relationship impacts every person-of-effort in the world: For all of those who are willing to work hard, there are always and only two things that are necessary to achieve success at anything: *vision* and *patience*....

## 7

## PRACTICE WHAT YOU PREACH

A clever little girl came running up to her father and asked, "Daddy, why does there have to be death?"

"All things must die, honey," her father replied. "Death is okay though, because it is a natural part of life; the more you can understand this now, the better you will be able to handle loss in the future."

"Okay, thank you daddy," the little girl replied. "Also," she continued, "I dropped your favorite coffee cup and it just died a few minutes ago."

*Live the message that you teach, and be prepared in every instant to have your resolve be tested, because it will be....*

8

## THE DIAMOND IN THE ROUGH

A day had passed since the village had been attacked and ravaged. Not much was left of it; the damage was immeasurable. Only a few people remained: a young boy among them. The boy wandered aimlessly in disbelief; he lost his hut and his family. He did not know where to go or what to do.

He saw a stranger appear out of the smoke. The stranger somehow seemed safe, seemed wise. The boy stood and stared at this man. The stranger was flipping a stone with one hand. Even in the pain, the sadness, and all the darkness, the boy could easily see that this stone shined brightly, and his eyes remained affixed on it.

The stranger motioned for the boy to come closer. When the boy was next to him, he flipped the stone again, and he watched the boy's eyes follow it as it rose and landed on the ground. The boy slowly reached down and picked up the beautiful, clear rock, and he never took his eyes off it as he handed it back to the stranger. The stranger asked him if he knew what it was, and the boy just shook his head indicating that he didn't.

The stranger told the boy that the stone was a diamond, and he gave it to the boy. "I see what's been done here," the stranger said, "and I want you to have this." The boy said nothing; he was still too numb to talk. The stranger knelt down next to the boy and said, "That stone was forged deep underground; farther down than you can imagine." He paused as the boy stared at the stone, then he continued, "It would have stayed down there, you know, deep in the earth... but something terrible happened. A great volcanic eruption took place that shook the world and left destruction in its path. But out of the destruction came this rock and others like it. Out of the deep destruction came something so solid and amazing, that nothing in the world is now tougher than it, or more beautiful."

The stranger smiled at the boy and said, "And now that is yours. I hope it can help you," and he turned to walk away. The boy reached up and grabbed the stranger's sleeve until he turned back around. "Here," said the boy as he handed the diamond back to the stranger, "I don't want it." The stranger was bewildered, but took the diamond back, stared at it, looked at the boy, and then said, "May I ask why not?"

"I don't want it," replied the boy, "because I want to become the diamond."

9

## THE COACH'S LESSON

A situation occurred, some things were said, and anger flew. Some people stormed out, others remained.

The coach gathered those who stayed, had them take a knee, looked them in the eyes, and began:

"The truth is it's disappointing that _____ would say something like that; the whole event was actually really disappointing... But let me tell you something that's a fact: People like that will come and go in and out of your life all your life. All your life. But The one person who will never go in and out of your life but will always be there, is you. You and you alone have to live with every single decision that you make. So every day of your life you better ask yourself, "Is this a decision I really want to make?" You better ask yourself, and I mean really ask yourself, "Is this a decision that I will be happy that I made a week, a month, a year, or even many years from now?" Because if it's not, you better stop, turn around, and make a better choice."

What he taught them applied far more reaching than the events that occurred that day, and for many, the coach's lesson stuck for a lifetime....

## 10

# MANY GURUS, FEW MASTERS

Finding a guru is easy. In today's world, a simple web search can help you find accessible gurus on every subject, in every area, and available to offer guidance to you through multiple modes of communication. In the Information Age, we certainly have no shortage of gurus. We do, however, seem to have a shortage of masters.

A guru spreads knowledge and imparts wisdom, which are certainly wonderful gifts; but a master has conquered the internal struggles of the human psyche. A master continually and comfortably rides into the depths of the unknown and lives from a place of constant congruence. We may need gurus to teach us at certain points in our lives, but we must become masters of ourselves.

Teachers can only take us so far, in the end, we must abandon our gurus' teachings, as well as our gurus themselves. We cannot abandon ourselves, however, because we are all we have. In the end, the reason gurus can only take us so far is that, ultimately, *no one can master you but you.* It may be true that there are many gurus in today's world, but it is also true that few have mastered themselves....

11

## RECALCULATE

My navigation system in my car is amazing. Turn by turn voice directions help lead me exactly to a desired destination. If I miss a turn, the navigation system does not complain, nag, or even tell me to make a U-turn; instead, the instant I miss a suggested turn, the navigation system immediately recalculates and suggests an alternative route, leading me from exactly where I am in that moment to my desired destination.

We all could learn a lot from navigation systems, and it's the same lesson that successful businesspeople all over the world frequently share with me: Forget about what "should have been done," and focus on the present moment. Like successful businesspeople, the best athletes in the world have what is called a "short memory" for mistakes. In other words, once something is finished (whether it's a business deal that didn't work or a play gone wrong), successful people do not think about what *already* happened, only what *can* happen.

The same can be true for you and me in our every day lives. When we encounter a problem, we can waste our breath talking about what "should have happened," or how things "should have gone," or we can simply eschew complaining in favor of brainstorming what we can do now. The past is gone. The future is hypothetical. The only thing that exists, the only thing that is real – is the present moment. In this moment and this moment alone, we have to develop a plan to get around/over/through the obstacles that are in our paths. Complaining will do nothing to solve our problems; neither will worrying.

We can talk about what it takes to be successful or we can just do it. Ultimately, for whatever obstacles we all face in this moment, there is only one thing left to do: Recalculate.

## 12

## TAKE THE TIME TO BACK IN

When you enter a parking space, you can either pull directly in headfirst or you can take the time to back into the spot. If you take the easier approach at first of just pulling right in, then later, when you leave, you will have to use additional effort to back out and turn around. If you take the time when you initially reach the parking space, however, you can back into it; then when it's time to leave you will be able to pull away with less effort.

Life is the same way. If you take the time to do the harder work first, things get easier over time. If you give in and take the easy path though, the road ahead can get very tough.

In life, we can either put the work effort in up front or scramble to make up for the lack of initial hard work. It's rare that people regret working hard. It's common that people regret not working hard enough. Take the time to back into the proverbial parking spaces in your life, and you will likely find things getting easier for you in the long run.

13

## HOW THE UNIVERSE TEACHES

Although most people understand that the Universe will present us all the lessons we ever need to know in this lifetime, what many do not know is *the way* in which the Universe teaches:

From the time we are very young, the Universe will present lessons to us. The first time lessons are presented to us, the Universe is gentle in the way It teaches. If we get the lesson, the Universe moves on to teach us something else. If we do not get the lesson, the Universe will continue to present that very same lesson to us time and again, and each experience will be more difficult than the last.

The goal of the Universe is not to hurt us, but to teach us. If we take the time to understand the lessons that are presented to us, we will be less likely to barrel headfirst into one similar mistake after the next. As long as we remain unaware of the method the Universe is using, however, we will likely continue to suffer. Learn what the Universe is teaching you the first time, and there will be no need for It to repeat the lessons.

## 14

# MY WIFE WON'T COMPLIMENT MY COOKING

In 14 years of marriage, my wife has never given me even one single compliment on my homemade soups.

After reading that statement, maybe you're thinking she's rude. Then again, maybe you're thinking she's just plain honest and my soup's just not good.

The truth is, however, I have never made any homemade soup.

We create assumptions quickly, and we run with them. Then, we become attached to our assumptions like they are a part of us. We even argue with others over them.

How absurd….

After all, assumptions are nothing more than unproven information.

Try not to make as many assumptions this week, or at least consider being a heck of a lot less attached to the ones you do make. Interestingly, if you do that, you might just also watch the way more peace will seep into your life.

Now, which way is that kitchen anyway? I think I'll try to make some...

time to sit down and enjoy whatever delicious food my awesome wife made today.

What? You didn't assume I was going to say "soup," did you?

15

## FOCUS ON THE LIGHT

It happened many eons ago that the Divine Source traveled throughout the world generously spreading seeds across the land. Each seed was given a small portion of the Divine Light.

The first day the seeds landed in the world, they faced a harsh rain that punished them, but they talked to each other about the radiant Sun that legends said would come to save them. The next few days, they saw no such sun, however, only cold winds and dark clouds. The seeds began to complain. They whined amongst themselves about how the world was harsher than they expected. Some of them even wished aloud that they were never born.

Only one seed among them was not like the rest. This seed felt all the same harshness that the others felt, but she saw no reason to complain. Instead of waiting for this "grand sun" that she heard so much about, this seed turned inward to try to bring the light out.

She focused on her own light, and she pushed hard against the ground. Her roots began to sprout. All along the other seeds told her what a waste of time it was to try to do anything about her predicament. This seed, however, saw no need to feed the negativity, and she continued in her quest to bring the light out. While the other seeds continued to grumble loudly, she focused on pushing her roots in the ground.

The complaining the other seeds did eventually faded into the background as she concentrated more and more on what she could control. Eventually, she heard nothing else but the sound of the universe. She worked so hard that she could feel her circumstance change. At once, she sprouted through the ground and towards the sky. As she looked up, the clouds parted and the sun shone brilliantly on her! It was better than she had imagined.

Though her fellow seeds had all perished in their misery, the heroine of the story learned the great secret of the universe: The Divine Light is inside all of us.

We can listen to others tell us how miserable the world is, or we can turn inward and trust the Divine inner voice to describe what we experience. The choice is each of ours to make, but regardless of circumstances, make no mistake about it: The seed of light is there.

## 16

## MASTER COMPLAINER SYNDROME (MCS)

Master Complainer Syndrome (MCS) is a real condition that I just made up. It is serious, toxic, and can be a direct cause of misery. This condition can be longstanding, but luckily, there are ways to identify MCS and correct it.

It is true that people suffering with MCS play lots of manipulative games with others, but they tend to make excellent use of two manipulative games in particular: The "YES, BUT..." game and the, "IF IT WEREN'T FOR YOU..." game.

The YES, BUT game involves agreeing with some type of negative assessment of yourself, only to turn around and justify why you are doing whatever it is you are doing. *"Yes, I know I did that, but I had to because..."*

The IF IT WEREN'T FOR YOU game involves placing blame on others for why you do not accomplish what you believe you could if they did not stand in your way. *"If it weren't for you, I wouldn't have to complain all the time."*

People with MCS are so good at these two manipulative games that they can actually even combine them with the phrase, *"I know I do "X," but you …"* and then they go on to put the blame on others.

People with MCS know how to justify and excuse anything they do. They regularly contribute to negative environments, and then they complain about those very same environments. Those with MCS do little positive for others, but when they do, they certainly let people know about it. People suffering with MCS do not look at their own faults except insofar as to point out others' mistakes. People with MCS tend to minimize the hurtful things they do to others, yet they have a wonderful ability to maximize the hurtful things that are done to them.

People with MCS are miserable to be around, most notably because they do not seem to have any awareness of how toxic their presence really is.

If you or someone you love is struggling with Master Complainer Syndrome (MCS), do not fret, there is help. The first step is recognizing that you complain a lot. The second step, and perhaps the more important step, is to *stop complaining*, because let's be honest, people hate having to listen to complainers. The ultimate cure for MCS, however, is to realize that complaining doesn't change anything; only action does.

17

## THE TRUTH IS EVER-PRESENT

*A long time ago, the master said to a group of people, "We are blinded by what we see. Whatever we see, we believe to be true. We interpret our fickle senses as accurate; we consider our beliefs to be reality. Some have said that more people are certain than in doubt; others disagree. I say that if you wish to see the truth, then do not be in favor of, or opposed to information. What you hope to see, you will; what you fear to see, you will. You never need to look for what is ever-present. Even the trees can shake what is left of their spirit, but you have no idea how to do so. Find comfort in the latter."*

*A troubled listener interrupted the master, "You are just saying words. Who could understand what you are saying? Tell me how you speak any truth!"*

*The master replied, "Who told this man I was speaking truth?"*

*But no one answered, and the angry man told the others they were foolish for listening, and then he headed on his way.*

*A student who had been following closely with every word that the master said then spoke up, "Master, what you have said makes perfect sense. I understood it all."*

*Knowing he had added statements that made no sense, the master smiled and said, "Here, my enemy and my friend have heard what they hoped to hear. Still, the truth is ever-present."*

What do you hear when others talk? You can hear the best of what they say or the worst; how you interpret your experience is up to you; but like the master said, the truth is ever-present.

## BUILDING STRONG NEURAL PATHWAYS

Neurons are nerve cells in the brain. There are a tremendous number of neurons in every person's brain (more than a hundred billion of them), and they communicate with one another through something called "neural pathways." Some neural pathways are strong whereas others are weak. The amazing thing about the strength of many neural connections is this: *It's actually up to us to determine how strong they are.*

Habits are strong neural pathways. The more you do something, the stronger the neural pathways. If you walk every day, your brain's neural pathways for walking become very strong. If you recite a poem often enough, the same thing happens. We have neural pathways for everything we do, including our attitudes. That means if you practice being positive, you will strengthen your brain's neural pathways for positivity. It also means if you practice pessimism and negativity, those too, will strengthen.

When it comes to things you want to accomplish but haven't yet tried, the neural pathways just aren't there. Once you begin to practice what it is that you would like to do, the neural pathways begin to develop. It's true that strengthening a neural pathway can be a challenge, but creating a neural pathway is easy. It begins to be there simply by observing others do what you want to do. It becomes stronger as you try to do it yourself. And it becomes an ingrained neural pathway (habit) once you have done it enough times.

How long or many repetitions does it take to build strong neural pathways in areas that you want? That's for *you* to find out, because it depends largely on *how badly you want it* and what you're *willing to do* to get it. The only thing I can encourage you to understand is this: With enough time and effort, creating the neural pathways you want can absolutely happen.

## ABSTRACT LOVER

Sometimes people fall in love with the *idea* of others. In those instances, people see and love their partner's potential, but in the reality of their presence, something falls short. Lovers like this struggle in relationships because they constantly hope their partner will live up to the idea they have created. When their partners cannot live up to the theoretical idea that they have formed of them, the abstract lovers are let down.

Abstract lovers are responsible for their own let downs, however, because their partners always were who they were. The lesson is that the projections we have of others are not always reality. In fact, it's rare that projections are ever entirely accurate. Therefore, in cases where people fall in love with the idea of others, their partners may not actually be hiding who they are at all; instead, their abstract lovers may simply be projecting inaccurately.

When you love your partner, you love your partner, mistakes and all. When you only love the idea of your partner, you become a nag, forever harping on your partner to be different. In your nagging, you become as unattractive to your partner as your partner is to you.

See reality. See your partner. Fall in love with who your partner actually is, and you might just find a deeper love than any mythical idea that you created in your mind….

## 20

## BE OPEN TO TRUTH

*A man returned from a long journey only to find that his house burned down. Not far from where the house was lay a corpse of a child that was burned beyond recognition, and the man believed it was his only son. After crying for days, the man cremated the body and kept the ashes above his mantle. He locked himself in his house and cried continuously for months.*

*One day his son (who had been kidnapped before the house fire) returned and knocked on his father's door.*

*"Who are you?" asked the father.*

*"I am your son," replied his child.*

*But the father did not believe the boy and refused to open the door. In this way his son eventually left, and this time he lost him for good.*

The man in this tale might seem foolish until we consider how many times you and I continually cling to our own beliefs. Unfortunately, the more rigidly we cling to our beliefs, the more we miss truth – even it if knocks on our door.

## MY TEMPER IS NOTHING

"Master," said the student, "I need your help. I have a terrible temper, and it troubles me."

"Fine," replied the Master, "Hand me your temper and I will help you with it."

"I cannot hand it to you," said the student.

"Why not?" asked the Master.

"Because it is not a thing," answered the bewildered student.

"If I hear you correctly, " replied the Master, "your temper is no-thing."

"That's correct," said the student.

"Well then," his Master asked, "If it is *nothing,* then how can you have it?"

"I guess I don't," replied the student.

So solves that.

When you understand that your anger is nothing but what you make it out to be in your mind, you too will have the power to change it and the potential to no longer be troubled by it.

22

## THREE PATHS

There were once three fish who, at different times, encountered the same shiny object at the bottom of their pond. The first fish came upon the object and fear shot through him. Something told him it was worth exploring, however, so he attempted to get a closer look at it. The object was behind a great many sticks and weeds that blocked his way, and he realized that he might end up doing a lot of work all for nothing, so he gave up and went on his way.

The second fish saw the same shiny object, but had no interest in it and kept swimming on his way.

When the third fish saw the object, he too felt the same fear and curiosity that the first fish felt. He also saw the great many obstacles in the path, but unlike the first fish, he viewed the weeds and sticks as a challenge, and pursued clearing them right away. He worked and worked and worked long after the other had given up, but still he did not reach the object.

The first fish swam by and told him he was foolish to pursue something that was impossible, and he told him to join he and all the other fish at the top of the pond for some easy eating. "There are worms just sitting in the same spot in the middle of the water!" he told the third fish, and he scoffed at him for wasting his time with all the hard work. The third fish did not want the easy meal because the object for him was his dream; so he stayed while the others left.

After a great deal of time and hard work, the third fish finally reached the object. He was elated to have reached his goal, but then his heart sank when he saw the object seemed impossible to open. "I worked so hard to clear my way to the object," the third fish thought. He didn't think he would have work to do once he reached his goal, but little did he know he was only halfway there at that point.

Alone, exhausted, disheartened, afraid, and with the other fish long gone, the third fish continued to work hard. He refused to give up, and eventually, long after he expected it to happen but still in the midst of his tremendous hard work, the object cracked open. Inside he found a lifetime supply of fish food. He knew then that dreams do not become fulfilled simply because we want them to be. He learned that hard work doesn't end when we think our goals should be met, and if we never give up, we can achieve anything. The third fish grew strong and large, and he lived well beyond his dreams.

23

## WATCH OUT FOR THE CONES!

Imagine if you put up construction cones in your house. Imagine if they were all through your house, maybe ten in each room. Imagine further that you encountered a penalty that led to an uncomfortable consequence each time you bumped into one of these cones. You would likely not be able to relax much in such an environment. In short, it would be miserable to have to constantly avoid the cones.

Taking the idea of cones a step further: What if each cone represented a rule about life that you made up? You could even write your rules on the cones: *"Don't say what I don't want you to say."* or *"Don't act in ways I don't want."* Or *"Don't think that."* Or *"Do think this."* You do, after all, have many unwritten rules just like this in your mind already.

The rules you have about how other people "should" be are pretty specific, but you either don't realize your rules, or you simply don't acknowledge them. When others break your unwritten rules, you get pretty upset; and the more attached you are to your rules, the more upset you get. You can even change your rules, and still you continue to get upset when others break them. But, a constant problem remains for you: It's impossible for everyone to learn all your ever-changing rules.

Imagine if you made your rules very clear for others by writing them down on cones for all to see. You could set up the cones everywhere for others to see. The exercise might be worth trying, because if you did that, you could learn several things

1. You could learn how many rules you do in fact have.
2. You could see how difficult of a path you make for others to take.
3. You could learn how rigid you are.
4. You could learn how much you set people up for failure.

All in all, setting up cones with your personal rules on them can teach you about you, and it can give others a clear picture of whether or not it is even worth it to attempt to be close to you. After all, the more cones you have, either the more you nag or the more you play the victim when others don't follow your rules. In either case, more cones equal less comfort for others.

Set up real cones up and tell people to watch out for them... or better yet, take them down – because very, very few people ever really want to be around the nagging disgruntled who are hard to please.

24

## DAILY WITCH HUNT

When we recall the horrors of 17th Century Salem witch trials, we might cringe at the senseless nature of what they involved. Though most of us would love to believe that we are more advanced than those who participated in witch hunts, the truth is that we are not. In fact, what you might be surprised to learn is that we have all gone on plenty of witch hunts already, and many of those occur daily.

A witch hunt occurs when *unfocused fear finds a target*.

Anxiety is fear's neurological twin, so it is not a far stretch to say that a type of witch hunt occurs when *misunderstood anxiety finds a target*. And how many times have we all, in states of anxiety, "created" problems with our loved ones in an unconscious attempt to understand our own feelings? In short, we all have taken things out on the wrong people at times, and usually our misunderstood anxiety finds the target of those who are closest to us.

The next time you find yourself on a witch hunt in pursuit of someone to take out your feelings on, remember you are acting in similar ways to the people of Massachusetts in 1692 – and instead of pursuing others to target, pursue yourself. When you look inward, you can find that a large reason you feel the way you do has to do with your own physiology (hunger, fatigue, stress, hormones, etc.) and psychology (level of assertiveness, esteem, ability to communicate, etc.). By looking inward, you might just find that what you learn about yourself is fascinating and intriguing enough to give up your daily witch hunts altogether.

25

## PLACE YOUR ORDER

A friend once told me that if you walk into a coffee shop and proclaim that you are thirsty, the barista will ask you what you want to drink. You will then have to place an order before your thirst is quenched. The concept is simple. Ask for what you want, but be specific.

Most people say they want to be successful. Most people hope that things can go differently in their lives. Most people want and hope for a lot in life. Although wanting and hoping are wonderful concepts, they are not as specific as placing an order.

What do you want in life? What exactly do you want? Figure it out, because if you can be specific, and I mean very specific, it will be much more likely to happen than if you simply metaphorically proclaim to be thirsty.

Oh yes, there is one more thing. Once the barista gives you your drink, you have to pay for it; that is, you have to do something besides order to get what you want. The same is true in life. Place your order from the universe. Be specific. And then, once your ordered has been clearly made, work incessantly toward achieving it – and no matter how tough it gets, no matter how big the obstacles are or how long it takes, never, ever give up.

## PRIME TIME

We see what we are primed to see. The moment we buy a new car, the odds are we will notice far more of that type of car on the road than the day before we got it. It's not just buying a new car that this phenomenon happens with, however, because that same concept applies to everything. If we go to a theater to watch a movie that unexpectedly turns out to be largely focused on pigeons, for instance, then on our way out of the movie, we are much more likely to notice many more pigeons than we did on our way into that theater.

*"Priming"* is a psychological construct that involves being prepared to see something. The following third grade joke between Kaia and her friend Jesse exemplifies priming:

Kaia: "Hey Jessie, spell the following word: S-I-L-K.

Jessie: "S-I-L-K."

Kaia: "Now say the word you just spelled out loud five times really fast."

Jessie: "Silk, silk, silk, silk, silk."

Kaia: "Quick: What do cows drink?"

Jessie: "Milk."

Kaia: "No silly, cows drink water."

Cows drink water, but Jessie was primed to say "milk."

Priming prepares our brains to see something. It is true that we can be primed from the outside; Kaia's joke is an example of priming from the outside. It is also true, however, that we can be primed from the inside; i.e., we can "prime ourselves." And we prime ourselves whether we realize it or not; but the most effective way to purposely prime ourselves is to be mindful of what we put in our psyches.

Imagine if your daily routine involved meditating on spreading peace to others. Imagine if your daily routine involved saying to yourself every single time you leave your house: "I will find opportunities to be kind today." The truth is we do prime ourselves; the unfortunate part of that truth is that we rarely realize how much we do. Everything we choose to surround ourselves with primes us. Everything we read, watch, and listen to primes us. How we spend our time primes us for every next moment.

So the question is: How do you use your time to prime yourself?

27

## THE POWER OF YOUR ENERGY

We are energy. Some of the energy we are is untouchable and beyond description, but the rest of it is largely determined by us. The part of our energy that we have the ability to influence is impacted by the foods we eat, the amount of sleep we get, the people, places, and things we choose to surround ourselves with, and what we tell ourselves.

What do you eat? How does what you eat impact your energy on a daily basis?

How much sleep do you get? Too little or too much, and your energy is not the same.

What do you surround yourself with? What comprises your environment? What statues, images, or lack thereof are you around most days? What kind of people do you invite to be near you? In what type of conversations do you engage? What kind of music do you choose to listen to? Where do you go?

Of your thoughts, which are yours versus which are others'? What type of self-talk do you have? Is it negative, positive, or neutral? Do you rely on extreme language ("That was terrible!" or "I can't believe that!"

or "That shouldn't have happened!" etc.) to describe your daily experiences?

Maybe we will never be able to control all of our energy, but we will always have the option to control at least the parts we can do something about. Pay attention to the foods you eat, the sleep you get, the environment (people, places, things) you are in, and your self-talk. Pay attention to all of it, and watch the power of your energy multiply in indescribable ways.

Observe and contribute well to the power of your energy, because whether you want it to or not, it reverberates through others more than you realize. Your energy *will* touch someone today. The question is: *What kind of impact will it have?*

## THE OMNISCIENT EGO

Our egos are our sense of who we are. They are designed to help us feel safe. Our egos tell us that what we know is accurate. They convince us that the information we have about the physical world and the metaphysical realm is complete. In short, our egos have us believe we are "right."

The Divine seems to be more vast than anything we can describe. Proponents of some religious faiths, however, tend to espouse that they can describe exactly what God is, and atheists use the same level of certainty to say exactly what God isn't; but in both cases, the egos of the believers and nonbelievers equally and alike tell them that they are "right."

The universe is filled with mystery. Our best scientific and rational knowledge has no logical or rational argument for the moment before the origin of the universe. The Big Bang theory is great and helps explain a lot; but ultimately, it is limited. It does not, for instance, tell us how something started from nothing, nor does it give us any information regarding the void into which the universe is expanding. There are limits to what we know, but our egos trick us into believing we can be certain about our knowledge. Belief, however, is a psychological construct. People believe without a doubt that there either is a God or isn't a God – and both sets of believers are convinced they are accurate. The omniscient ego convinces the human race that it is "right."

I've been fascinated to meet the devoutly religious and the devoutly atheistic. Both speak condescendingly toward others about the knowledge they believe is certain "truth." Both ultimately rely on what they experience as a "gut feeling" regarding the information they hold. Both represent two sides of the exact same coin.

The same is true of people with political beliefs, philosophical beliefs, and beliefs of every kind. Still, people argue, fight, and kill for the beliefs of which they are "certain."

The omniscient ego appears to drive the certainty with which people speak, and it seems to stifle any attempt to expand consciousness…. Or maybe it doesn't – I really don't know….

29

## TWO BROTHERS

This is the story of identical twins who were separated at birth. They grew up in completely different, warring lands and never knew anything about each other. Each grew up strong in body and mind. Each became prince in his respective land.

Despite the distance that separated them, the two brothers lived strikingly similar lives. Each brother was devout in his beliefs. Each was bull-headed and steadfast in what he knew. From physical traits to ability to intellect, each truly was identical. Each too, was filled with passion for impacting others. There was, in fact, a single, albeit extraordinary, difference between the two: One was a devout atheist, and the other a devout fundamentalist in his faith.

Both of the brothers eventually became king. They each ruled confidently, and they each wanted more than was given. As fate has it, the two brothers, unbeknownst to either, were destined to meet on the battlefield.

Their armies, equally matched and led, eventually encountered a standstill. The battle was to be decided as battles in that time and place usually were: with the kings dueling in a one-on-one fight. The moment arrived where they met for the first time. With their armies behind them, each took off his helmet. As you might imagine, each was shocked to see the other, and neither was prepared to slay the other, but ever-stubborn as they both were, each still wanted to be high king, so they decided to have a battle of wits to determine who the supreme ruler should be.

Though their intellects were identical and their knowledge vast, the battle came to a screeching halt on the subject of the Divine. Each was confused and flat out baffled how the other could not believe what he believed. It was clear the battle could not be settled by those present, so they sent for a wise man who lived in the mountains.

The wise man came before the kings and heard each of their amazing arguments. He commended both on their intellect and breadth of learning – and then he turned to leave. The kings, in unison shouted for him to stop. "Declare a winner!" They demanded. But the wise man simply turned to them, smiled and said, "You have both learned to have faith, and that is beautiful. One of you believes that the Divine exists, the other believes that the Divine does not exist. You each equally and passionately believe in something you cannot prove. Neither of you is right, yet if you come to know each other, you will find that you both are right." And the wise man left.

Years went by. All fighting had ceased the day the two brothers met. Peace reigned between the countries as the kings arduously attempted to figure out what the wise man meant. With each passing day, the brothers came to know each other more and more. Regardless of the difference in beliefs, the brothers grew to be best friends; they were happy to be reunited, they were kind to all they met, and they found that they focused much less on being attached to what they thought they knew.

And then one day, in the exact same moment, both brothers realized the wise man's message: It didn't matter what they believed. It only mattered how they lived, what they did with their lives; their actions were the truth that made them both right.

And the story of the two brothers is a story for all of us. Believe what you will. Every thought about something we cannot know for sure is a belief – and beliefs abound. But regardless of what any of us believe, in the end, it is our actions the world will see … And it is our actions *from this moment forward* that matter most.

## 30

## THE PLURAL PRONOUN CHANGES EVERYTHING

A talented and troubled young man found the guru at long last. He knew the custom of asking the master a question, and he was prepared to find out what he wanted to know. He approached the seated guru and said, *"I struggle, and I don't know why. I try and try, but no matter what I do, I cannot seem to achieve my goals. I am alone. I strive and I fail, and I do not understand. I want to know. Can you teach me?"*

The guru sat in silence for a bit with an austere look – until he broke into a loving smile. When he spoke, he had the young man's full attention. *"When you change your mindset from the singular pronoun "I" to the plural "we," you can see that you are a part of something greater. Understanding this, you will come to know that you are never alone. You do not fail, either, in anything you do. You merely trek a path. Nothing, either, is impossible for the "we." Every individual can do everything that everyone in the history and future of the world can do because we are also that person. We are everyone – as are you. Understand this much, and you will be free."*

Upon hearing the guru's words, the young man was

liberated instantly, and in that moment, he saw the history and future of the world flash before him. He was now a part of all that he had met, and equally a part of all that he had yet to encounter. He understood he was everyone. He, the "we." We all are….

The plural pronoun changes everything.

## 31

## WET THE SAND

Physicists have recently hypothesized that the ancient Egyptians may have used a unique technique to move the giant stones across the expansive distances to build the pyramids. They believe that the technique involved wetting the sand in front of the giant stones as they slid them on given contraptions across the desert. There could not be too much water, or that would have made the delivery difficult, and the sand could not be completely dry either. There was, in effect, an optimal level of water needed to carry the enormous stones. If this hypothesis is correct, it provides us with an answer to one of life's great mysteries.

Even if this theory turns out to be inaccurate, however, the thought brings to mind another amazing answer to one of life's other great mysteries; a mystery that impacts us all on an individual level: how to achieve our own personal dreams. Setting out to accomplish our dreams takes every ounce of effort we have, but perhaps the key is in the middle path of balance. Too much of one thing is excess, too little is deprivation.

The sand represents the obstacles in front of our goals. Wetting the sand in front of our goals entails preparing for the obstacles that we'll encounter. Wetting the sand might involve things like working harder than we ever imagined to make things happen, or maybe it entails not repeating mistakes. When we wet the sand at the optimal level, we learn how to respect the balance of life. Wetting the sand in many ways entails working smarter, not harder. Because the sand represents the obstacles we will encounter, the more we prepare for them, the better chance we have at getting over them.

The pyramids were built with monumental effort, and so too, are our dreams achieved with colossal energy. Figure out how to wet the sand in your life; because even though the task you set out to accomplish can seem overwhelming, by wetting the sand, you will make your dreams achievable. And what you do by living out your dreams can be as awe-inspiring and lasting as the pyramids....

32

## YES, BUT...

*"Yes, I know that's the better thing to do, but here's my excuse for why I'm not going to do it...."*

In the classic "Yes-but" game, everything before the "but" is essentially a bunch of hot air. We say "Yes" in an attempt to fool others (and sometimes even ourselves) into believing that we understand, and then we say "but" and follow it with an excuse to rationalize why we're not going to do that (what we know is best) anyway. In other words, after we say "but," we describe how we really feel. Sometimes, of course, we just say the "Yes" part to placate others, and then we follow the "but" with what we really want to tell them.

We play the "Yes, but" game to convince ourselves that what we are doing is "right," even though we absolutely know that we are not. The fact is that change is hard. We often would much rather take the easy way out (i.e., believing we already have the answers) than take the more difficult and vulnerable path of realizing we have so much more to *learn.*

*Yes,* you probably know all about this phenomenon already, *but* nonetheless you are invited to be a little more mindful of the ways in which you rationalize the ineffective or harmful things you do this week….

## 33

## YOU ARE NOT A PINK ELEPHANT!

If someone called you a "pink elephant" in a derogatory way, would you get upset? Honestly?

If you said *"Yes,"* that you would get upset, then you have a lot of work to do on yourself (unless of course, you actually are a pink elephant, in which case, please accept my apologies).

If you're like most people, however, you probably said *"No."* Why is that? Why would you not get upset at someone calling you a "pink elephant?"

Because it's absolutely ridiculous, that's why. It is beyond ludicrous to think that you are a pink elephant – but even more simply than that: you would not get upset if someone called you a pink elephant, because, well, it just flat out isn't true.

So follow this: if you *wouldn't* get upset if someone called you a pink elephant because you know *it simply isn't true*, then why get upset at *anything* anyone says about you that also isn't true?

You are not a pink elephant. You are also not anything else that you're not. So consider not getting upset at things that people say about you that are not true. You will likely save yourself a whole lot of heartache, and in the end, you will find much more peace.

34

## HALF A CRACKER'S NOT ENOUGH

And so I heard...

*There once was a frugal, but hungry man who looked around for something to eat. He found seven crackers and began to gobble them up. When he got to his last cracker, he split it in half. After he ate the first half of the seventh cracker, he realized he was full – and then he became angry. "If I would have known," he thought, "that all I needed to eat was a half of this cracker to become full, I never would have needed to eat the first six crackers. What a waste!" And he spent the rest of the day complaining....*

As absurd as this scenario might sound, every time we either complain or altogether discount the experiences that have led us to this exact moment, we are doing the very same thing. "Why did I waste my time doing 'X' when I obviously didn't need to do that?" we might ask. Well the answer is simply this: we cannot merely eat half a cracker and be full.

Life has led us to this moment, and whatever 'mistakes' we made en route to this moment were not mistakes, but experiences; experiences that led us to where we are right now. When it comes down to it, we can either dwell on what we "never needed to do," or we can accept *what is as what is*, and recognize that we needed every experience we ever had to teach us what we know in this present moment. The more we understand this, the more prepared we will be for the innumerable opportunities life offers us to expand our consciousness.

35

## SLINGSHOT

Rare are the people who can say their lives have gone exactly as planned. Instead, most of us are led to believe (either through experiences or imagination) that our lives will go one way, only to be swept off our feet and moved in entirely new directions. Accidents, injuries, deaths, circumstances, and effort all steer the course of our destinies.

Sometimes in the midst of what feels like defeat in our lives, we get the sense that we are somehow "moving backwards;" and backtracking away from what we believe is our destiny can be painful. Mistakes, rejection, and what we perceive to be "negative circumstances" can all lead to a feeling of emptiness, an idea that our dreams are now broken, and a sense of defeat.

Overwhelming challenges in life can sometimes lead to our wanting to cry out, "I feel like I'm taking two steps forward and four steps back!"

Defeat, however, does not have to be the only reason we appear to be "moving backwards." There may be entirely different reasons our lives our headed in what seems like the "wrong direction."

Consider the rock that is pulled back on a slingshot –
"Why am I moving backwards?" it might ask; not
realizing that it is being set to be projected farther than
it has ever gone before. Similarly, it might just be in the
paths of our own destinies to, at times, "go backwards"
– with the very real purpose of preparing us to fly
forward and rise higher than we have ever gone….

The next time your life "pulls you backwards," be
mindful that it could very well be the universe's way of
preparing to slingshot you to an amazing place:
somewhere more beautiful than you could ever
imagine….

36

## SMALL-MINDED FOOL

*There once was a small-minded fool who believed every rumor he heard. He took every article he read about public figures at face value, and he even vigorously argued with others regarding the veracity of what little he read and knew. This small-minded fool judged others he never met. He opined about what he believed to be truth, merely because he heard it rumored or saw it written somewhere. Even though this small-minded fool only ever had part of any given story (not all sides unedited), he ran with what he heard and read and spread his ignorance to others.*

*Then one day, sometime down the road, this small-minded fool made a mistake of his own that was written about (albeit incompletely). He ran around telling others that he was so much more than that simple mistake he made – but it all fell on deaf ears. You see, this small-minded fool could not convince others that he wasn't the things they read or heard about him, because he lived in a land where all the people were taught to form strong opinions based on only a few interactions and very little information. And so he spent the remainder of his days alone and unhappy.*

Now what I take from this tale is this: It's a good thing you and I don't live in such a land where we have learned to make judgments and condemn others based off what we hear or read (or after only a limited number of interactions) – because if we did, we might also be ignorant, small-minded fools....

37

## THE WEIGHT OF ATTACHMENT

The Master said:

*Two travelers embarked on grand adventures. Each had to cross many obstacles en route to their destination. Near the end of both journeys, the travelers came to the Great River.*

*Neither traveler had means to cross the river, but each, in his own way and with tremendous effort, was able to obtain a raft.*

*To this point, both travelers' voyages were fairly similar. Once they crossed the Great River and landed on the other side, however, their paths differed significantly.*

*The first traveler thought about how long and hard he worked to obtain the raft, and he could not bring himself to let it go. Thus, he held onto it, tugging and pulling it through forests and mountains, until the weight and burden of it inhibited him from going any further. The first traveler never reached his destination.*

*The second traveler, however, left his raft on the bank of the river the moment he landed on the other side. He then continued light-footed until he reached his destination. He recognized that the raft was only intended to help him for part of his journey.*

Those who understand that the rafts are *beliefs* will be free from the weight of attachment.

38

## UNNECESSARY ANGER

A man pulled off to the side of the road because something was wrong with one of his tires. When he opened the trunk of his car, he saw that he didn't have a tire iron. He looked around and noticed he wasn't far from a farmhouse, however, so he walked toward it in hopes that the person living there would have a tire iron.

Along the way, he started to think, *"This is so much farther than I thought,"* and *"He might not even have a tire iron,"* and *"What if he has one, but doesn't want to be bothered?"* and *"He probably won't even open the door for a stranger,"* and *"This is a waste of time!"* He thought negative thought after negative thought until he finally arrived at the door of the farmhouse. He rang the doorbell, but he couldn't stop his negative thoughts from escalating and making him angrier and angrier. By the time the farmer opened the door, the man just screamed out, *"You can keep your stupid tire iron!"*

This story is humorous and seems a bit ridiculous until we reflect on the innumerable times we have gotten angry with others for no real reason at all. How many of us create problems in our own minds and then look for those problems to be played out in the real world? We imagine that the world *should* be the way we demand it to be, then we suffer by remaining trapped in our own angry minds.

The intelligent are aware that they create unnecessary anger; but the wise are those who let go of the unnecessary anger in their lives.

39

## ONE-MILE MARATHON

Change is absolutely possible. Whatever goals we set our minds to, we can certainly accomplish. Simply setting our minds to something, however, does not equate actually accomplishing it. Therefore, before we attempt to make monumental changes to behavioral patterns we have practiced for years, it might be helpful to align our expectations with the reality of what change will likely entail. To not do so, or to believe that change *should* or *will* be easy, is like attempting to run a one-mile marathon.

Imagine a person who has never exercised before setting out to run a marathon. Imagine still if the person would say after the first mile, *"Running a marathon is easy!"* We might all be fairly skeptical of whether or not that person truly understands that running one mile is not the same as running five miles or ten, or even fifteen or twenty, let alone twenty-five miles or the last and dreaded twenty-sixth mile.

A marathon is 26.2 miles. Running the first mile sets us on the right path, sure, but it does not really give us an accurate idea of what it is like to finish the entire race. Likewise, when we make a change in life, it might help us to understand there is no such thing as a *one-mile marathon*. The more we understand this, the better prepared we can be for the new path we have made a commitment to take.

Set out to run a proverbial marathon (or even a literal one), by all means, because what you put your mind to, you have the potential to accomplish. Change can happen, but be mindful to not believe in a one-mile marathon, and you will be one-step closer to actually achieving the goals you set out to complete.

40

THE BOX

When my daughter Kaia was 5 years-old, she brought home a pamphlet that someone handed her. The pamphlet said "This is the truth." Kaia asked what that meant. "This must be true, right daddy? It says, 'the truth'." So I took her to her playroom and set up a box. I had her lie on the floor so that she could only see one side of the box. I then had her close her eyes while I took four different objects from her playroom, and I put one object on each side of the box.

I told her to open her eyes, and told her not to move (this way she could only see one side of the box). Next, I asked her what she saw. "I see a My Little Pony."

I said, "Now do not move. Is there a My Little Pony on every side of the box?" She said, "I don't know."

I said, "Why don't you know?" She said, "Because I can only see one side."

I said, "Is it true that My Little Pony is on the side you see?"

She said, "Yes."

"So it is truth," I said, "that My Little Pony is there. But is it also truth that knowing that tells the whole story of the box?"

"I don't know," she said.

Then I had her move to where she could see two sides of the box. She saw a book against the second side. She could now see the book and the My Little Pony character. I asked her what she saw and she described it. I then asked her again if that was the whole story. She said "no," and that she now believed she only had part of the story.

Then I told her, "The people who wrote that pamphlet and the people who follow that way see one side of the box. What they see might very well be truth to them; but it is not likely the truth of the entire box. And then I quoted the opening lines of the Tao Te Ching (which, in all fairness, she already had memorized a year prior). "The Tao that can be told is not the Eternal Tao. The Name that can be named is not the eternal Name."

"What people can describe as the Divine cannot possibly encompass the entirety of that which is truly Divine," I went on. "Throughout your life, people will claim to know the truth; but be mindful that what they see is only their side of the box. For your part, you should know that there are multiple sides to the box. There are even multiple ways to view the box from above and below, inside and out. Therefore, live your life in a way that humbly remains open to understanding that in this incarnation, you will not likely know the entire box."

That is how I introduced my daughter to the idea of religion. And if you only see part of the box, you will likely disagree with what I taught her – and that is perfectly okay with me, because I know all too well that I do not see the whole box….

**41**

## DON'T DRINK POISON!

A man who was not living in accord with his True Self approached a guru. The man told the teacher that he was not happy. He said that he knew he was living the wrong way, but he did not believe he could change things. He felt stuck in his routine and in his habits, and he was certain his fate was now determined.

The guru sat in silence for a time, then told the man the following story:

*There was once a man who drank three poisons every day. He constantly consumed these three poisons, though he never believed they would hurt him. He imbibed them in the forest, he imbibed them in the mountains, and he imbibed them on the beach. One day, after drinking too much of the poisons, he became trapped in a shell. He lived the rest of his days locked in this shell.*

*If you are not careful, you too, will suffer the same fate.*

*The three poisons he drank are greed, hate, and delusion. The shell was his body.*

*If you understand this much, you will be free to find your own fate.*

The instant the guru finished telling the story, the man was enlightened. From that day forward, his habits and routine became forever changed….

42

## WAKE UP!

After he dreamed of the mountain and the teacher, the traveler searched for years until he found the place. He rested one night before his ascent. Though the years had worn on him, somehow, with renewed determination, he left his weariness behind and climbed until he reached the top of the mountain. He found the guru the dream told him he would find.

His heart raced – pounding swiftly from the hike, the anticipation, and the excitement. He knew the custom: the guru only taught when the student asked a question. He had prepared his question for years and the moment to ask it had finally arrived.

"What is God?" he asked.

"Why did you come here to know God?" The master replied.

"Because I want to know God."

"But you do know God."

Bewildered, the student said, "I don't even know what God is."

The master paused, peered right through the traveler, and gave a stern reply, "Then why do you seek something that you don't even know about?"

The student was taken back and with defensiveness replied, "I do know some about God."

"Tell me what you know about God, then," demanded the teacher.

The traveler replied with assertiveness, "I know that God is love. I know that God is a Presence. I know that God is probably in all things."

"Tell me more…" commanded the guru.

With forcefulness, the traveler said, "I know that I probably never needed to leave my house or even my room to know God. I know that this journey never needed to take place for me to understand. I know that God was, is, and always will be. I know that you are God, but so too, am I. I know that God is in all things animate and inanimate, and that every expression of love is an expression of God's compassion. I know that I have the ability to exude the compassion of the Divine in any given instant, should I choose to do so. I only need to recognize. I only need to awaken."

"Then awaken!" the guru sharply replied as he snapped his fingers.

And the traveler awakened... in his own home, in his own room, in his own bed. Never having moved a muscle or done a single deed for this journey, he realized he was in a dream within a dream when he did not understand, and he was awakened when he did.

And so it is for all of us....

43

## GRAVEYARD ROBBER

He took everything of value from the dead without ever touching a shovel. He was brighter than you know; because the truth is he had no one else do his bidding either, yet without magic, he took everything he wanted. In short, he was the wisest thief among them all. He was so good that he could even take from the dead with a clear conscience, because even though he took without permission, what he took, the dead wanted him to have.

He was the graveyard robber of knowledge. He took the wisdom of the deceased. He read every book he could, because it is in the books where the deceased leave their ideas. He listened openly to every story, because it is in the stories they told with their actions while living that the dead can convey their wisdom.

Most people go to their graves without passing on what they know; but many others do. The greatest minds we know about either wrote their ideas down or lived such powerful lives that others wrote about them. We never even have to learn to read or write if what we do can impact others profoundly enough.

It would be a shame to not rob the wisdom from the graveyards throughout the world, but three important questions exist for the graveyard robbers: What knowledge have you taken from the deceased? How have you used the knowledge you gained? And perhaps the most important question to be asked is this:

How will you live the rest of your life from this moment forward so that others deem your own grave worthy of robbing?

## 44

## TAKE DOWN YOUR STICKY NOTES!

John served ten years in a state prison for attempted murder. Before this last prison sentence, he had been in and out of incarceration for years. He has most recently been out for three months, and he now has a place of his own. All in all, he has had a very hard life. John says that he doesn't believe in a "higher power," but he actually does: his higher power is "respect." John never wants to be disrespected, and he takes great measures to ensure that. Unfortunately, John has been setting himself up for failure for years — That is, until he discovered something invaluable that is slowly changing the way he thinks....

Ten years of incarceration impacts a person, and John was institutionalized. In prison, you have to understand, there are more rules than one can count. There are rules that the authorities implement, and there are rules that inmates have on top of those rules (for a group of people who don't like rules, it's actually pretty interesting how many rules inmates make for themselves). The rules the penitentiary makes can be left behind when a person leaves the prison walls; the rules the inmates make stay with a person much longer.

The most important rule that inmates enforce with each other is to follow the Rule of Respect. Allowing oneself to be disrespected in prison can equate torture or death, so by default, respect begins as a High Deity of Necessity – then, over time, it morphs into the High Deity of Habit.

The moment John was released from prison and moved into his new apartment, he put sticky notes up throughout his entire house to make sure that any guests he would have would follow his rules. *"Take your shoes off!"* was the first sticky note visitors would see when they walked in. *"Don't pee on the seat!"* was a sticky note that could be found in the bathroom. *"Don't make a mess on the sink!"* was above the mirror in the bathroom and on the window in the kitchen. *"Don't put your feet up on the coffee table!"* was in the living room. *"Don't do this!"* and *"Don't do that!"*: the notes were everywhere…. John told me that he needed to be "very clear" with people so no one disrespected him.

John had literally made tangible rules to his *god of respect*, and he wrote them out for anyone to see on bright yellow sticky notes. The problem, as we all know too well, is that as soon as we make rules for people to follow, we simultaneously create opportunities for people to break our rules. The more rules we create, the more chance we provide others to break our rules. But perhaps more importantly, the more rules we create, the more we unrealistically expect that the world *should* be the way we demand it *should* be, rather than learning to see *the-world-as-it-really-is*.

For John, he made his rules concrete by putting them on sticky notes. For most of us, however, we make arbitrary rules in our minds and simply expect others to "see" our rules. Like many others I've worked with through the years, John didn't like having to serve the *god of respect*; but unlike many others, John was absolutely ready to change. He was motivated enough that he was willing to follow the one directive I offered him: "*Take down you sticky notes.*" When he did, a change occurred. The world began to disrespect him much less – not because the world did anything differently, but because John learned to see the world for what it is: not good or bad, right or wrong, respectful or not, the world just *is what it is*. Most people don't usually set out to "disrespect" others; instead, the majority of people simply tend to act in ways that maximizes their own pleasure and minimizes their own pain.

John took down his sticky notes and is beginning to change his life in profound ways.

What rules do you have arbitrarily written and stuck to the inside of your mind? Whatever they are, I'll offer you what I suggested to John: Take down your sticky notes. The change just might amaze you….

**45**

## THOUGHT-SHAPED MIND

Recent brain scan research has demonstrated that a particular area of our brain (left temporal lobe) is activated when we read stories; and then, for a period of time afterwards, that same part of the brain remains heightened. In short, brain experts have been able to scientifically confirm that *what we take in stays with us*.

Now many people might say that we really didn't need fancy scientific machines to scan our brains to learn that what we take in sticks with us, and let's face it: they're probably right.

But now that we do have that concrete scientific information, think about this:

The next time you watch a horror movie, ask yourself if you really want that information in your psyche. The next time you sit in front of a "kill-em-all" video game, think: "Is this really what I want my brain to be processing?"

Does filling our brains with violence shape us? Of course it does. Whatever we fill our brains with impacts us.

The famous philosopher Epictetus once reportedly said, "As you think, so you become." Even before Epictetus, the great spiritual teacher Buddha said, "All deeds are led by mind."

But famous philosophers, spiritual leaders, and scientific information aside, you yourself know from life experience that what you take in sticks with you. So think about what you want, but recognize that the part of your brain that you choose to activate will likely stay activated for awhile.

Maybe it's important for us all to be mindful this week of what we choose to fill our brains with, because *what we choose to see is what we choose to be*.

## 46

## 22°F IS BOTH WARM AND COLD

One day in the winter of 2014, with the wind-chill factor, the temperature dropped to negative 40°F. The day after it hit that low, the temperature went up to 22°F. I walked outside on both days, and I noticed a difference. The day it was 22°F, I thought, "It seems warm today." The reason it seemed warm: There was a 62° difference in temperature, and relative to the -40°F, 22°F seemed warm.

The following week the temperatures rose back up to about 50°F. Then, fickle as the weather is in Southwestern PA, the temperature sank back down to 22°F. This time I thought, "It's freezing outside!"

22°F is both warm and cold, depending on the comparison we make.

So far, the lesson doesn't seem very profound. That is, until we begin to look at our problems in the same way. Seen one way, whatever is troubling us on this day might be overwhelming; but seen from a different vantage point, our problems might just become very manageable.

What were you angry about as a child? Don't

remember? Has time changed your perspective? In retrospect, was it worth being as angry as you got? What about the problem you're facing today? How will it look in 5, 10, or even 20 years?

*Compared to perfect pleasure, even a minor discomfort can seem major.* Compared to the vastness of an ever-expanding universe that we cannot comprehend, however, our problems seem minimal.

Ludwig Wittgenstein once said that there are no real problems, only problems in language. What language do you use to describe your troubles? Language from one angle might make 22°F seem cold; but language from another angle might make 22°F seem warm.

What temperature do your problems feel like? Better yet, with the right perspective, what temperature can you *make* your problems feel like?

**47**

**PURSUING JOY**

*Adapted from the Katha Upanishad*

Once a man was near his deathbed. To ensure his passage into heaven, this man decided to sacrifice a certain number of animals. The man's son, however, did not believe that hurting animals would bring his father to heaven, so he offered to sacrifice himself in place of the animals.

Now Death himself was extremely impressed with the sacrifice offered by the young boy, so he offered the boy any three boons he desired. After the first two wishes were made and accepted, the boy asked if there was *"anything beyond death."*

Death tried as hard as he could to persuade the boy to choose anything other than that knowledge. He offered the boy every earthly desire, but the boy refused them all, and wished only to know if there was anything beyond death. Death was so impressed with the boy choosing wisdom over every other physical pleasure that he told him the great secret:

"Only those who follow the path of joy will find fulfillment. Every pleasure ends; only joy is eternal.

Those who seek and find peace in their senses and heart, right concentration in their minds, and who abandon all untruths, will find life beyond death."

And so it is to this day: When we chase temporary pleasures, we find that they have a psychological death; but when we pursue joy and the ineffable experiences that accompany it, we find that eternity is right in front of us.

Joy cannot be found in the ego, but the True Self. Joy is not in physical pleasures, but in psychological ones. Joy does not come with "being right," but in being happy. Joy is a deep spiritual fulfillment, and even pursuing joy can bring peace.

## "ALMOST ENLIGHTENMENT IS NOT "ENLIGHTENMENT"

A water buffalo jumped through a window. His horns made it through, his neck made it through, and his body made it through – but his tail got caught in the window. He did not make it all the way through the window. He was close, but he did not finish.

"Almost enlightenment" is not "enlightenment."

It can be difficult to fail. It can be devastating to lose something we have worked for and desire. Failure can lead us to feeling overwhelmed and believing we might as well give up. We might try for years to gain wisdom that seems to remain ever-elusive; but *trying to gain that wisdom* and *actually gaining it* are two different entities altogether.

Maybe every obstacle that has gotten in our paths has been there for a reason. Maybe holding on a little longer is exactly what we all need to do. Maybe, like the buffalo, we are one instant away from achieving what we are seeking; and maybe, just maybe, what we need to do is keep trying.

It can be overwhelming to not be where we want to be in life, but my guess is that it will be more overwhelming if, at the time of our death, we look back and see that we gave up. Just because something seems impossible doesn't mean that it is. We all have to find a way to keep moving forward despite any obstacle because "almost enlightenment" is not the same as "enlightenment."

## GOING TOO, INDIANA

My wife and I have had our dog Indiana since January of 2001. He was 14 years old when he died. He was an awesome dog.

Death can be tough to cope with, but the reality is the bell tolls for all of us, and it is not romantic or idealistic. Death is hard and painful and inevitable, and not much can ease the pain that we feel when we lose a loved one.

Indiana was scrappy and loving and faithful. He loved my wife, daughter and I unconditionally, and I think we all could learn a lot from that.

How is it, after all, that as a species, we have gained so much consciousness, yet we seem to not be able to touch the unconditional love that dogs give us?

Death brings reflection, but so can life. Most of us have made countless mistakes and either intentionally or inadvertently hurt others along the way. Whereas it is true that we cannot get back a single instant of the moments we regret, what we can do is strive to be better in every waking moment from this minute forward.

Like it or not, we will all cease to be. While we are alive, however, we never have to cease trying to be better people. We can be more kind, more forgiving, more compassionate, and more accepting of others and ourselves.

We are all going too, Indiana. Here's to hoping that we can strive to be as faithful, loving, and unconditional as you were….

## 50

### THE ASTRONAUT

He got out of bed early – he hadn't slept much that night. He was hungry, and he felt agitated and was being irritable toward others. His thoughts were negative and spiraling to worse….

Then he remembered his training for spacewalks around tall satellites. In space, there is no "up" or "down." To reorient himself in space if he ever felt afraid while he walked along the outside walls of skyscraper-sized satellites thinking that he was "too high up and would fall," he simply closed his eyes, and saw himself walking horizontally rather than vertically. By closing his eyes, in a brief second, he reoriented, and his new view of it all changed everything.

This morning, too, everything seemed to be spiraling in a negative way – maybe not in fear of falling, but in agitation, discomfort, and anger….

And then…

He closed his eyes….

In a moment, he reoriented himself. This time he didn't allow his hunger, agitation, irritability, or negative thoughts to consume him. Instead, in the instant he closed his eyes, he thought of everything for which he was grateful. Like concentric circles expanding, his gratitude grew and spread.

And his new view of it all changed everything….

## MASTER CRAFTSMAN

I have a lot of wonderful memories from playing different sports throughout my life, but I will never forget the best summer of baseball I ever experienced. My brother had just returned to the area after he spent six years in the Oakland Athletics minor league farm system. The two of us had a blast all summer playing ball together. Maybe the most memorable moment came from me watching his first at-bat in that league, though, because the lesson from I got from it reaches far beyond any sport.

When my brother walked up to the plate for his first at-bat in our summer league that day, he did it so smoothly that he seemed to not even move the dirt under his feet as he took his batting stance. With grace and calmness, he watched the first five pitches go by until he had a full count (3 balls and 2 strikes). Then, as the sixth pitch approached the plate, with pure muscle memory and no thought, he rocked back with the greatest of ease and swung effortlessly. He sent the ball not only far over the right field fence for a homerun, but also over the road behind the field and over the trees behind that road. Every moment of it was amazing to watch.

Besides still being able to recall the sound of the ball screaming off the bat, what I remember most was how smoothly he did what he did. There was seemingly no effort as he made the act of hitting look so simple. How could something so amazing be so easy? The answer is that he had spent years upon years practicing hitting, and he was a master craftsman at it.

Watching people master their craft can be inspiring, but it can also be disheartening. It's inspiring when it evokes a spark inside us to find and master our own crafts; it's disheartening when we see people master the wrong crafts.

Whatever we practice long enough, we master. For the majority of my professional career, I have spent a great deal of time with people who are in dark places in their lives. They see the awful side of life, and they choose to continually focus on it. They focus on what they don't have, who they're not with, and every obstacle in their path. They spend minutes after hours after days after years telling themselves all about the negatives that exist in the world and in their own lives. Essentially, what they do is *practice negativity*. They practice it until it becomes so smooth and so effortless, that without thought and with the greatest of ease, they now live what they have practiced every day.

Whatever we practice, we strengthen. We are all
master craftsman. Our crafts are what we do and even
what we think. What is your craft? Is it a physical task?
Is it a job or a role you play? Or could it be,
unfortunately, the craft of negativity itself? Because if
you dedicate yourself to your craft: you will get very
good at it – even if what you practice is negativity....

52

## DON'T SIGN FOR THE PACKAGE!

When a package is delivered to your home and a signature is requested, that does not mean you *have* to sign for it. In fact, if you do **not** sign for the package, eventually it will be returned to the sender.

Sometimes we might not want what people send us — so why do we sign for it?

A wise person taught that if a giver gets someone a gift and the receiver does not accept the gift, then that gift still belongs to the giver. In the same way, if a person attempts to project anger, jealousy, or hatred onto you, and you do not accept those things, then the anger, jealousy, or hatred remains with that person.

The next time someone tries to give you anger, jealousy, or hatred, do not "sign for the package." Regardless of how difficult it might be to do, do **not** accept it. When you do not accept it, the anger, jealousy, or hatred remains with the one who is attempting to give those things to you.

Anger, jealousy, and hatred do not bring anyone peace. Eventually, the sender of these things will have to learn how to either deal with them or let them go. By not accepting them, however, it is no longer your issue to confront.

In fact, if you do not want what comes with any of the negative energy of others, do not sign for the package in which they send it.

## 53

## INCESSANT

Never stop. Whatever you pursue, pursue it fully. Throw yourself into all you do and live your life to the fullest every day. Be incessant about learning, growing, and becoming.

Exercise. Work on your physical health. You have one body; take care of it.

Read. Work on your mind. The more open you are to new knowledge, the more your mind can expand. Work on learning about your mind. The only person you live with every moment of every day of your entire life is you; so take the time to know yourself.

Meditate. Work on your spirit. Practice listening to the stillness, and you will attain indescribable benefits.

Love. Work on your relationships. You are not alone in this world and your actions impact others. Take the time to consistently evaluate the role you play in relationships irrespective of what others do, and then make the effort to change the things you need to change.

Inspire. Work on your creativity. You have unique gifts,

and when you don't pursue developing them, a part of you feels absent. Use your talents every day.

Master. Work on the ways in which you handle your emotions. Master yourself, but understand that it will take incessant drive, determination, and openness to do so.

Never stop. Whatever you pursue, pursue it fully. Throw yourself into all you do and live your life to the fullest every day. Be incessant about learning, growing, and becoming.

# ABOUT THE AUTHOR

Christian Conte, Ph.D. is a licensed professional counselor, nationally certified psychologist, and an internationally recognized expert in the field of anger management. Dr. Conte is the author of several books and videos, including: *Advanced Techniques for Counseling and Psychotherapy*; *Life Lessons*; *Zen Parent, Zen Child*; *The Anger Management Workbook*; *Keys to a Better Life*; *The Art of Verbal Aikido*; and *Getting Control of Yourself: Anger Management Tools & Techniques*. You can learn more about him at www.DrChristianConte.com or find him on Twitter @Dr_Conte.

CPSIA information can be obtained
at www.ICGtesting.com
Printed in the USA
LVHW030125020322
712389LV00005B/165